THIS BOOK BELONGS TO:

....

START DATE:

....

PRAYERS

TO HELP

YOU THRIVE

DEVOTIONS
TO HELP WOMEN
LIVE WITH JOY & CONFIDENCE

ZONDERVAN

Prayers to Help You Thrive
Copyright © 2023 by Zondervan

Portions of this book were excerpted from the NIV *Devotional Bible for Women: Fresh Insights for Thriving in Today's World.*

Requests for information should be addressed to:
Zondervan, 3900 Sparks Dr. SE, Grand Rapids, Michigan 49546

Zondervan titles may be purchased in bulk for educational, business, fundraising, or sales promotional use. For information, please email SpecialMarkets@Zondervan.com.

Cover design: Michelle Lenger
Interior design: Emily Ghattas

Contributors: Chike Chukudebelu, Katie Hardeman, Margaret Hogan, Denise Hildreth Jones, Shauna Niequist, Tsh Oxenreider, Rachel Randolph, and Alece Ronzino.

ISBN 978-1-400-33511-4 (hardcover)
ISBN 978-1-400-33940-2 (custom)

Printed in Bosnia and Herzegovina
23 24 25 26 27 28 GPS 6 5 4 3 2 1

Contents

INTRODUCTION

The idea of what it means to thrive is truly unique to the individual. To thrive to flourish, to grow strong. For you that man mean feeling good about life, being at peace with who God made you, or experiencing contentment even amid struggle. Even though we all have a different definition of what it means to thrive, the biblical concept of rejoicing is at the core.

Life doesn't always go our way, and in those times you may not feel joyful. The world is full of cancelations, changes, and a great deal of pain. But the apostle Paul reminds us to be joyful in all things and to rely on God rather than on circumstances (1 Thessalonians 5:16–18).

And what is the best way to rely on God in all things? It's invest and work to create a meaningful relationship with him. This interactive book is an invitation to grow and thrive—in your life and in your faith walk. This beautiful mix of devotions, Scripture, prayers, and prompts will help you develop or strengthen your time with God. The topics include areas of relevance to women today, such as social justice, economic equality, and social media addiction. But other topics are universal in their importance, such as prayer, fasting, decision-making, and relationships.

You can work through this individually or invite friends, family members, or your small group to join. Process each section at whatever pace works for you—daily, every other day, weekly, or monthly. After you read each entry, ask God what he wants to say to you. Ask him what he wants you to learn. What does the Lord want you to dwell on longer or to do in response to what you have read? Then listen quietly for his answer.

Our prayer is that this resource will lead you into a deeper relationship with the God who loves you and wants you to thrive.

How to Use This Book

Read the entry. Highlight words, phrases, or Scripture references that speak to you. Take notes in the margins.

Read the prayer. You can pray aloud or silently. If God speaks to you, write it down. If you have additional prayers of your own, feel free to write them in this space.

Respond to the reflection prompt. If you're completing this workbook as a group, you can write down additional thoughts people share.

After you've completed a section, record how everything is going. This will serve as a check-in with yourself and help you progress on your journey to thrive.

Different and Not So Different

SHAUNA NIEQUIST

I once did a study on Exodus, which is not the kind of Bible study I'm used to. The other people in the study spoke Greek and Hebrew. I speak French, which is slightly less helpful in matters of theology, although much more helpful in fine dining and shopping. I feel good about the trade-off, generally, but this study made me reconsider.

What surprised me is that I found myself very connected to the story of Exodus. It's a great story, a big, sweeping story about the sea and the desert and the sky, but it's also a story of incredibly fine detail, like a Fabergé egg, like a large painting with teeny tiny brushstrokes. And as much as it's a very important story about big themes and pervasive truths about the nature of God and his people, a finely wrought web of ideas and ideals, it's also about blood and bones and midwives and frogs and fires and bread.

Maybe these details matter to me because even though so much of modern life and theology insists that what matters is my mind, my soul, my inner self, my heart, there is still this nagging part of me that knows on some deep level that the things we see and touch and hear and taste are spiritual too. The dichotomy between spiritual and physical doesn't make sense to me because so much of God's work in my life has been the repairing and stitching together of the two.

There is still this nagging part of me that knows on some deep level that the things we see and touch and hear and taste are spiritual too.

It didn't make sense to the Exodus writers either. The olives and the wine and the ideas and the stones and the mountain and the soul all matter deeply and signify something important, instead of the ideas and the souls being truly important and the rest just being props on loan from the theater department.

Exodus brought to the surface and brought to life this little part inside me that whispered, "I thought so! I hoped so!" I think the best stories always do that, always resound somewhere below our stomachs with a sense of rightness, a sense of congruence with the way we were made and the way we understand ourselves.

On the mornings that we studied Exodus, I felt myself walk through the rest of the day differently. I felt like my life, my actual daily, water and wine and blood and guts life, was a little ennobled, like I could stand up a little straighter. I ate my hummus and bread and olives at lunch feeling like I was a part of something old and elemental, like eating good, fresh food made by someone's hands was something important. It made me think about the

yarn of my scarf, how someone made it with their hands, and how threads and garments and colors mattered so much when they built the ark of the covenant.

It made me feel like even though a million things are different in my life than they were then, like email and Gore-Tex and Zone Bars and dishwashers, some things are not so different, like bugs and yeast and the impulse to worship. There's still a big story, disguised as regular life, and the big story is about love, death, and God; about bread, wine, and olives; about forgiveness, hunger, and freedom; about all the things we dream about and all the things we handle and hold. Exodus was the Wild West, lawless and risky, and it's the cities we live in, bursting with life and meaning, and someday, when the future brings a world we can't even imagine now, Exodus will be there, in the songs and sounds and in the flesh and bones of a people who still wander and yearn for home.

Some things are not so different.

PRAY

That you will see your own life differently in light of your time spent studying the Bible.

That God will reveal how your story is connected with the bigger Story.

REFLECT

What parts of Exodus resonate deeply with your daily life?

Lord, help me to see the
majesty in the mundane,
the glory in the
grittiness of the daily,
the story you're writing
in even the smallest of
details in my life. I praise
you for every moment.

MONTH   DAY   YEAR

GOD SIGHTINGS

SCRIPTURE I AM MEMORIZING

WHAT AM I LISTENING TO?

Artist:

Song:

Playlist:

WHAT IS HAPPENING IN MY LIFE?

WHAT IS HAPPENING IN THE WORLD?

Stop and Remember the Truth: You Are Enough

ALECE RONZINO

I see beauty all around me. It's in the trees, lit as though on fire when the setting sun hits them just right. I see it in the steady rhythm of the waves, greeting the shore only to say goodbye again. I find beauty in majestic mountains, tulip fields and the awkward grace of giraffes in motion. I recognize it in the joy-filled eyes of the poor, and in the expressions of sheer wonder on the face of a toddler. I see beauty in a meal prepared with love, and a home opened wide with welcome and warmth. I find it in the vulnerable and brave sharing of hearts.

I see beauty all around me. But I can't see it in the mirror.

I pray that I will see
your holy face reflected
in my own today, that
I will treat myself with
the same gentleness,
kindness, and
compassion that you
long for me to know.

The picture I have of myself, tucked way down in the deep recesses of my heart, has long been distorted. A lifetime of feeling not enough has crumpled that internal photo into a torn, tattered and ugly mess. No matter how hard I try, being enough has always felt far beyond my reach. And it's nearly impossible to see beauty where insufficiency is all that's visible.

My view of me has been warped, as though I'm seeing my reflection in a carnival mirror — blurry and disfigured.

Over the past several years, that core belief of my own inadequacy was reinforced even more. My husband's 18-month affair with my friend shouted that I wasn't desirable enough. When he left me after 10 years of marriage, I heard that I'm worth leaving more than I'm worth fighting for. And when he told me on his way out that he didn't love me and probably never had, it reiterated that I'm not valuable enough to be loved.

What little remained of my self-image shattered into a million tiny pieces. The roots of insufficiency burrowed even deeper, strengthening their death grip on my heart.

I am not enough.

My journey since then has been long and arduous. Losing my marriage ultimately also meant losing my ministry, the nonprofit my husband and I had founded together in Africa. My whole life changed drastically as I moved back to the States and started over in every way imaginable.

Like the aftermath of a tsunami, all I could see in my reflection was the broken, messy, ugly devastation of my life. And I couldn't help but question how there could possibly be beauty in all that rubble.

While it took a while to get there, my journey has begun taking me down new roads of healing and restoration. When I quiet my heart and lean in, I hear God's ever-gentle words of reassurance, affirming that I am enough. My perfectly good Father makes no mistakes, needs no second drafts and declares me beautiful exactly as he made me. I am enough because he is enough. He is my sufficiency. He is my adequacy. He is my enoughness.

So even while I may still struggle to see beauty in the mirror, I am learning to see it revealed in his eyes.

Though I continue to struggle daily to see myself through his eyes, God has been lovingly restoring my heart. With grace and gentleness, he continues to reveal glimpses of his image of me, which is slowly reshaping the picture I have of myself.

I've learned that a healthy self-image can only come from staring long and hard into Jesus' face. I catch my true reflection solely when I see myself in his eyes.

It's there that I see that I am enough because he is enough. It's there I see that I am desired, valued and fought for. It's there that I see that he recklessly loves the beautiful, imperfect mess that is me.

So even while I may still struggle to see beauty in the mirror, I am learning to see it revealed in his eyes.

PRAY

That you will increasingly see yourself as reflected in God's loving
eyes.

That you will learn to embrace and appreciate your own beauty,
inside and out.

That the distorted internal picture you hold of yourself will
transform into a true reflection of who you are.

REFLECT

What truth of how God sees you do you need to dwell on today?

MONTH DAY YEAR GOD SIGHTINGS

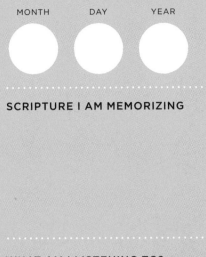

SCRIPTURE I AM MEMORIZING

WHAT AM I LISTENING TO?

Artist:

Song:

Playlist:

WHAT IS HAPPENING IN MY LIFE?

WHAT IS HAPPENING IN THE WORLD?

Then the Lᴏʀᴅ God formed a man from the dust of the ground and breathed into his nostrils the breath of life, and the man became a living being.

GENESIS 2:7

God Isn't Afraid to Get Down in the Dirt

ALECE RONZINO

The story of creation is an incredible one. For so many reasons. But mostly—at least for me—because it shows so beautifully the unmatched worth we have in God's eyes.

God spoke everything into existence, which is a whole mind-blowing thing all on its own: "Let there be . . ." and there was.

God was balanced between time and eternity—forming galaxies, zebras, mountains, and starfish with his very words. He spoke, and they were created. Something out of nothing.

When it came to his creation of humankind, however, he changed things up. Instead of speaking us into existence, as he did with everything else, he chose to form us in his own image.

I close my eyes: "Fearfully and wonderfully," he made us (Psalm 139:14). I've seen pictures of some pretty amazing sand sculptures, but I'd say that God's takes first prize.

And then he breathed into us.

Face-to-face, we inhaled his exhale. Our first breath came from the very mouth of God. I cannot even fathom the worth—the wealth—of that breath of life.

When my life is a mess or it feels like there's no end in sight to the challenges I'm facing, it's easy to think that God is far removed from it all. When the nights are long and the darkness closes in, his presence doesn't always feel very present. But just as he was with Adam in Genesis, he is right here in the dirt with me.

Regardless of what I feel, he never leaves me.

Regardless of what I feel, he never leaves me. He never forsakes me. He doesn't just watch me from afar; he sits right down in the messy chaos with me.

When I remember that he made me in his image, it's easier to trust that he is intimately involved in my life, even when I can't see him. And it makes me want to open my eyes wide and look for him in unexpected places.

Like right here in the dirt.

PRAY

That you will remember to look for God where you normally don't expect to see him at work.

That you will feel his presence in new and intimate ways.

That you will experience his matchless love and let that overflow onto those around you.

REFLECT

In what unexpected places can you see God at work right now?

God, you are close, as
near as my own breath.
Today, I pray that I
will reach out for your
hand and embrace
your presence in each
moment.

MONTH   DAY   YEAR

GOD SIGHTINGS

SCRIPTURE I AM MEMORIZING

WHAT AM I LISTENING TO?

Artist:

Song:

Playlist:

WHAT IS HAPPENING IN MY LIFE?

WHAT IS HAPPENING IN THE WORLD?

"For God knows that when you eat from it your eyes will be opened, and you will be like God, knowing good and evil."

GENESIS 3:5

Who's Writing Your Story?

DENISE HILDRETH JONES

In Acts 3, Peter and John encounter a man who is lame. Peter heals the man, and the people who see the man running and jumping are astounded. But Peter says to them, "You killed the author of life, but God raised him from the dead. We are witnesses of this. By faith in the name of Jesus, this man whom you see and know was made strong. It is Jesus' name and the faith that comes through him that has completely healed him, as you can all see" (Acts 3:15–16). Peter calls Jesus the "author of life." In Hebrews 12:2 we also find that Jesus is called the pioneer and perfecter of our faith. This means that he not only authors our journey of faith but also completes it. He is writing our life's story from beginning to end. So, why is it that we so often doubt God's ability to write our stories? Why is it that we often find ourselves trying to "help him out" as if what he desires to write isn't interesting enough, isn't fancy enough, isn't . . . well . . . enough?

Most of the challenges of our faith and our relationship with God can be traced back to the battle of faith that began in the garden. The Author had written the story, the ultimate love story. He had let Adam and Eve know that for their story to work in the perfect way he had planned and written, for them to enjoy this intimate relationship of evening walks and authentic conversation, something had to be written out of it: a tree. Just one tree. They could have everything else around them. Nothing was off limits for them but that one thing.

And in came that lie from the serpent that penetrated their hearts: "For God knows that when you eat from it your eyes will be opened, and you will be like God, knowing good and evil" (Genesis 3:5). Lies like this always target our hearts, trying to lure them into believing something about God that is not true.

And as they did, the story changed forever.

And this lie that changes the entire course of how the story was to be written targets Adam's and Eve's hearts to believe that God hadn't written their story well enough, that he was holding out on them in some way. They sadly would believe it, take the pen in their own hand, and write the story they wanted to be written themselves. And as they did, the story changed forever.

Immediately their eyes were opened to life in a way God had never intended.

Adam and Eve would now encounter a world and a story he had not planned on them having to endure. And their shame was great. The open, alive, intimate, loving relationship they had with God was now severed by their sin. All because they didn't like the way God desired to write their story.

This isn't any different from how Satan targets us. He loves to attack us with lies to penetrate our hearts about how God desires to write our stories. He accuses God of holding out on us. He accuses God of not making us good enough, talented enough, pretty enough, desirable enough. And then he dangles the pen in front of us and says, "Why don't you give it a try? Why don't you write your own story?" And often we take the pen and try to create the person we want others to think we are.

Our stories have such brokenness in them. The brokenness of our past. The trauma of our childhood. Who wouldn't want to whitewash the sordid details and create a completely different story for others to read? But when we try to write our own stories instead of trusting the ultimate Author, we will find ourselves trapped in hearts of performance, having no idea who the real us is. Authenticity goes out the window and in come the costumes we use for our charade. And the ultimate tragedy is that all this moves our hearts farther and farther from that intimate, cool-of-the-day love relationship with our Father.

God has made you enough.

God has made you enough. He has authored you well even in the chapters of your pain. And he is in your story if you can trust him with it. Let go of your desire to write it for yourself. Guard your heart from believing any lie about your Father. And remember why the Enemy wants you to think your story is not enough: because your story and the blood of the Lamb are the two things that defeat him! "They triumphed over [Satan] by the blood of the Lamb and by the word of their testimony" (Revelation 12:11). Our testimony is the story God has written on our hearts. And look at its power! Oh that we may never underestimate again the power of our God-authored story.

PRAY

That you will be able to recognize lies from the Enemy and guard your heart from them.

That you will find at least one safe person with whom you can share your whole story.

REFLECT

What pieces of your story have you felt God got wrong and have been tempted to rewrite?

Some days the enemy feels so strong, but I know you are stronger. And I know you are writing my story for good. Help me to trust you today.

MONTH   DAY   YEAR

GOD SIGHTINGS

SCRIPTURE I AM MEMORIZING

WHAT AM I LISTENING TO?

Artist:

Song:

Playlist:

WHAT IS HAPPENING IN MY LIFE?

WHAT IS HAPPENING IN THE WORLD?

David was thirty years old when he became

king, and he reigned forty years.

2 SAMUEL 5:4

Love, Grace, and Healing at Just a Touch

ALECE RONZINO

The woman bled for 12 years straight. Physician after physician shrugged his shoulders. She'd given up all hope of ever getting better. But then she heard about Jesus: the miracle worker. Desperate, she knew she had to get to him. As she clawed her way through the crowd, she carried much more than her illness—she carried shame. Like a bag of stones over her shoulder, she dragged along a heavy burden of rejection and fear. In some Bible translations, she's referred to as a woman with "an issue of blood," but her issues ran much deeper than that because her physical ailment made her an outcast in her own culture. Her emotional hurts and scars were likely far worse than her physical ones.

Finally catching up to Jesus, she reached out and frantically, yet gently, touched the hem of his robe. Immediately, she was healed. Jesus turned around and faced the crowd. "Who touched my clothes?" he said.

The passage says that she "told him the whole truth." She explained why she had touched him and how she had been instantly healed. Jesus cared enough to listen to her story. The long version. He just let her talk. He was on his way to heal a dying girl. People were rushing him. Pressing him. Insisting he keep going before it was too late. He silenced them long enough for her to tell her story.

The greatest healing wasn't the miraculous cure of her incurable disease; it was the passionate healing of her heart.

When she finished talking, he responded by calling her "daughter." It's the only time recorded that he addressed someone that way. The love she felt in that one simple word must have been overwhelming. After she poured out her heart, he responded with pure affection.

If Jesus' aim was simply to heal this woman's physical condition, he would have kept walking after she touched him, for she had been healed instantly. If that was all he was concerned about, he wouldn't have stopped, turned around, asked the question. He wouldn't have looked straight at her, talked to her, listened. But he did all those things. He wanted to let her talk. To tell her story. He wanted to call her "daughter." For that is when her heart was healed. He wanted to heal more than her body; his aim all along was to heal her heart.

I can picture Jesus looking her in the eyes as he talked to her. And making her look into his. The healing began as, face-to-face, his love was visible, and it resonated within her soul. His love broke through with a simple gaze, a listening ear and undivided attention.

It wouldn't have helped if he healed her physically but left her to still carry the hurt from her 12 years of uncleanness and disgrace. Despite her physical healing, might she have stayed holed up in her house? She was used to cowering, dragging her bag of shame behind her. But as Jesus looked into her eyes, he saw the woman he created her to be, and he wasn't content to leave her drowning in her pain.

The greatest healing wasn't the miraculous cure of her incurable disease; it was the passionate healing of her heart. God's primary concern is still the condition of our hearts. Physical health and a blessed life pale in comparison with a restored soul. God's heart hurts for our hurting hearts.

And he's called us to love just as deeply. Our accomplishments, ministry achievements, and external successes matter little compared to how we love others.

God still brings love, grace and healing through just a touch of his garment. We just need to remember that we, his followers, are now the hem of his robe.

PRAY

That you will understand that Jesus wants you to be whole.

That you will listen to others' stories, the long versions.

That you will look for opportunities to love others completely.

REFLECT

Where do you need healing—physical, emotional, heart-wise?

Lord, I want to see my purpose, my next steps, now. I pray that you will grow patience in me, that I will remember in moments of uncertainty that you walk with me in dark places, you set a path before, and that you hold my days in your hands.

MONTH DAY YEAR

GOD SIGHTINGS

SCRIPTURE I AM MEMORIZING

WHAT AM I LISTENING TO?

Artist:

Song:

Playlist:

WHAT IS HAPPENING IN MY LIFE?

WHAT IS HAPPENING IN THE WORLD?

Pushing Back Pride

MARGARET HOGAN

A fear and revenge cycle is hard to stop. When I experience this trap, I find myself at my most basic, human nature. For example, while studying theater in college, a "friend" stole the concept of my senior thesis performance, which I'd been developing for months, used it to stage her own show, and then won an award. Behind my anger was an intense fear that I would never be seen as significant, coupled with a huge desire to make this person pay for her offense. I entertained countless imaginary scenarios where justice was finally served.

The truth is, I rarely act on my impulses for revenge, but I have no problem indulging these fantasies in my heart. Fear is paralyzing, and revenge is consuming. They take up too much of my energy and eat away at my spirit. Worse yet, if I am sinning quietly, in the privacy of my own heart, I rarely have the good fortune of being found out and subsequently led kindly back to the cross, which is to say, saving grace.

So when I read parts of Genesis—Cain killing his own brother (4:1–16), Noah cursing his son's son (9:18–25), and the tower of Babel (11:1–9)—I can't help but let out a familiar sigh of resignation. The deep ache for wholeness, usually marked by some act of depravity, has been finding its way into our story since the first juicy bite out of that tempting fruit in the garden of Eden. I want to read these stories like I did as a child, and say, "Whoa, people were so terrible back then." But as a grown woman, I have seen enough life, tasted enough reality, had my heart broken enough to know that time has not made us better. As it was then, it is now: our human family is stuck in a rut. Look at current events, look at the relationships in your life, look at the shaky parts of your own heart. It's there. And it often shows up as that fleeting, sneaking feeling that maybe you do know better than God. You have a better idea than God's plan for you and all his rules. I believe we call this pride. And I believe it is at the root of the majority of our sin.

> I have seen enough life, tasted enough reality, had my heart broken enough to know that time has not made us better.

We bought into a lie that being created in the image of God wasn't enough. We weren't content to be like God and to be with God; we wanted to be God. And it didn't take much—just the suggestion that God was keeping something from us.

What we thought would satisfy left us naked and ashamed. That's usually how sin works.

Cain was jealous of God's favor on his brother. Noah was ashamed that his youngest son caught him naked and drunk. People gathered together and decided to do something amazing for the sake of being famous. Sound

familiar? So maybe you didn't kill your sibling for being your parent's favorite. And maybe you didn't lash out at your grandchildren to spite your son. And maybe you haven't schemed up some plan to bring glory and fame to yourself. Or have you? Have you hurt someone you loved because they got something that should have been yours? Have you been so ashamed that instead of facing the truth, you blamed others and made them pay? Have you spent your life chasing things that would bring you attention, adoration, praise?

I practice surrendering so that I can start again.

I've found that sin loves to keep us limping around the same block, day after day, week after week, year after year. When I find myself once again trembling with fear or seething with anger, I know it's time to recalibrate my insides. I ask myself, What tiny, secret ways do I believe I know better than God? What is it I really need? The answer almost always involves letting something go. Unclenching my fists, breathing and letting God be God. This is how I practice surrendering, so that I can start again.

PRAY

That you will honestly look into your heart.

That God will remind you to let go of your fears and desire for revenge.

That you will remember God is bigger than anything else.

REFLECT

How are you trying to be God in your own life?

Surrendering is so difficult. And waiting, forgiving, and trusting your timing in all things. Lord, please soften my heart today and help me to loosen my grip. I trust you. Amen.

MONTH   DAY   YEAR

GOD SIGHTINGS

SCRIPTURE I AM MEMORIZING

WHAT AM I LISTENING TO?

Artist:

Song:

Playlist:

WHAT IS HAPPENING IN MY LIFE?

WHAT IS HAPPENING IN THE WORLD?

Then the king summoned Ziba, Saul's steward, and said to him, "I have given your master's grandson everything that belonged to Saul and his family. You and your sons and your servants are to farm the land for him and bring in the crops, so that your master's grandson may be provided for. And Mephibosheth, grandson of your master, will always eat at my table." . . . Then Ziba said to the king, "Your servant will do whatever my lord the king commands his servant to do." So Mephibosheth ate at David's table like one of the king's sons.

2 SAMUEL 9:9–11

Bring It All to the Table

SHAUNA NIEQUIST

There will be a day when it all falls apart. My very dear friend lost her mom. That same month, another friend's marriage ended, shot through with lies and heartbreak. A friend I hadn't talked to in ages called late one Sunday night to ask me how to get through a miscarriage. "The bleeding," she said, "has already begun." As I write, a dear family friend lies in a coma in a hospital bed.

These are things I can't change. Not one of them. Can't fix, can't heal, can't put the broken pieces back together. But what I can do is offer myself, wholehearted and present, to walk with the people I love through the fear and the mess. That's all any of us can do. That's what we're here for, the presence, the listening, the praying with and for on the days when it all falls apart, when life shatters in our hands.

The table is where we store up for those days, where we log minutes and hours building something durable and strong that gets tested in those terrible split seconds. And the table is where we return to stitch our hearts back together after the breaking.

We live in a world that values us for how fast we go, for how much we accomplish, for how much life we can pack into one day. But it's in the in-between spaces that our lives change, and the real beauty lies there.

The table is about food, but it's also about time. It's about showing up in person, a whole and present person, instead of a fragmented, frantic person, phone in one hand and to-do list in the other. Put them down, both of them, twin symbols of the modern age, and pick up a knife and a fork. The table is where time stops. It's where we look people in the eye, where we tell the truth about how hard it is, where we make space to listen to the whole story, not the textable sound bite.

The table is the great equalizer, the level playing field many of us have been looking everywhere for.

We don't come to the table to fight or to defend. We don't come to prove or to conquer, to draw lines in the sand or to stir up trouble. We come to the table because our hunger brings us there. We come with a need, with fragility, with an admission of our humanity. The table is the great equalizer, the level playing field many of us have been looking everywhere for. The table is the place where the doing stops, the trying stops, the masks are removed, and we allow ourselves to be nourished, like children. We allow someone else to meet our need.

PRAY

That you will take the time to invite others to the table.

That you will be open to stitching others' hearts—and yours—
back together.

REFLECT

With whom do you sit at the table?

Help me to slow down, Lord. It is so easy to get caught up in a frenetic life of busyness, distraction, and activities and to forget the goodness, the growth, and the gifts you bring in shared slowness and in shouldering our burdens together. Help me to open my table up more and more often as I listen for your voice.

MONTH   DAY   YEAR

GOD SIGHTINGS

SCRIPTURE I AM MEMORIZING

WHAT AM I LISTENING TO?

Artist:

Song:

Playlist:

WHAT IS HAPPENING IN MY LIFE?

WHAT IS HAPPENING IN THE WORLD?

Do not seek revenge or bear a grudge against anyone among your people, but love your neighbor as yourself. I am the Lord.

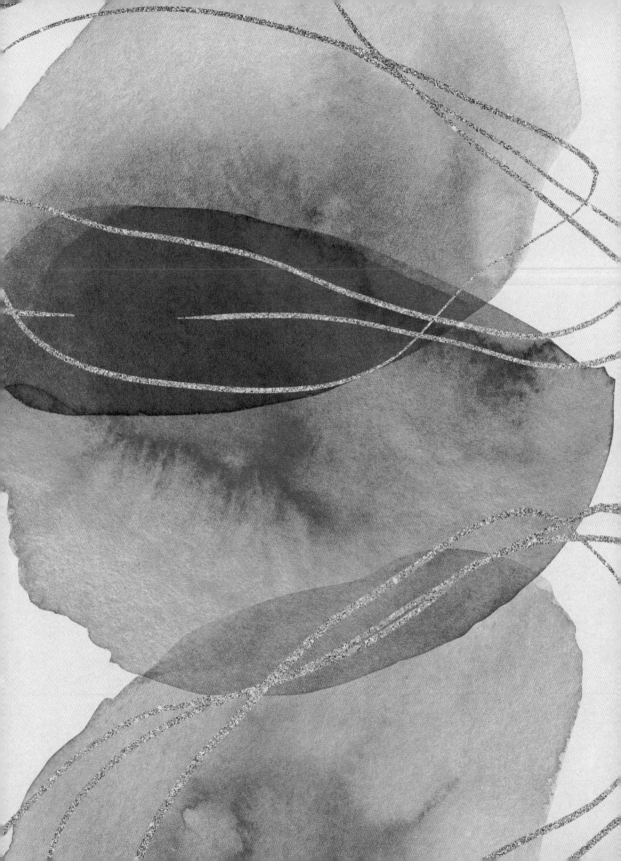

The Trouble with Holding Grudges

KATIE HARDEMAN

I was a senior in college when my dad was unjustly fired. He quickly forgave his boss because he trusted God would use the situation for good, but I had a much harder time forgiving. I was taking a self-defense class at the time, so I imagined what I would do if I ever crossed paths with his boss. I'd lie in bed at night, grinding my teeth and stringing together the perfect words I thought would sting the worst—right before I thrust my open palm to his nose. It's one thing if someone wrongs me, but if they hurt the people I love, the anger that boils in my heart surprises even me. I would never actually hit someone, but my continual daydreaming about revenge was dangerous for my heart.

Throughout Scripture God warns against such daydreaming. As the designer of the human heart, he knows what can poison it, darken it, and turn it from him. So he instructs his people to "not seek revenge or bear a grudge against anyone among your people, but love your neighbor as yourself" (Leviticus 19:18).

So many readers of the Bible prefer to stay in the New Testament, where Jesus also preaches this command to love your neighbors. But it is important to note that the character and purpose of God have never changed. He wasn't a God of wrath in the Old Testament and a God of love in the New Testament; he's always been both.

He has always instructed us to protect our hearts from bitterness and unforgiveness. He has always called us to love our neighbors and to love those who are hard to love. These are our "enemies," and these are our neighbors.

We obey because he is God, because he knows what is best for our hearts.

Immediately following God's command to love your neighbor as yourself, he says, "I am the LORD." It's as if he knew we would struggle to follow this command and would need a constant reminder of why we should obey. We obey because he is God, because he knows what is best for our hearts. He knows that the anger and bitterness that feel so right and justified at times are actually poisonous and destructive. And he knows that by forgiving and letting go of grudges and dreams of vengeance, we are choosing to protect our hearts from darkness.

PRAY

That God will help you to see these people as he does.

That God will reveal the dark corners of your heart where anger and bitterness may be festering.

That God will help you forgive and even bless those who are hard to love.

REFLECT

Who are the people in your life who are hard to love, and how has your heart responded to them?

MONTH   DAY   YEAR

GOD SIGHTINGS

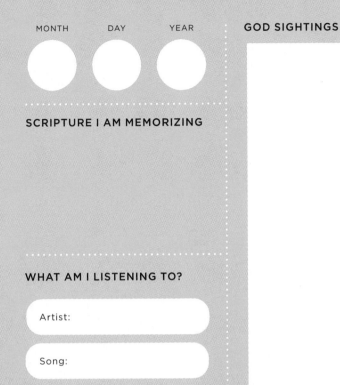

SCRIPTURE I AM MEMORIZING

WHAT AM I LISTENING TO?

Artist:

Song:

Playlist:

WHAT IS HAPPENING IN MY LIFE?

WHAT IS HAPPENING IN THE WORLD?

I don't want to live under the weight of a cloak of bitterness. Lord, please help me to shrug off the unforgiveness in my heart and to reach out in love, as you have loved me.

Choose to Go to God First

RACHEL RANDOLPH

I was feeding our new baby in the living room one day while my husband, Jared, got dinner ready. He wanted to make my homemade ranch dressing, but I hadn't yet written down the measurements for my "little of this, little of that" recipe. I offered to talk him through the steps from the rocking chair. Imprecision unnerves my by-the-book husband, but he hesitantly agreed to give it a go. I coached him while holding my sweet, milk-drunk baby in my arms, "Okay, chop up a handful of parsley . . . yes, that's enough . . . yes, wash it first . . . chop it a little finer . . . perfect . . . now add a little onion powder, lots of cracked pepper . . . a little more . . ." When I thought the dressing might be done, I asked him to bring the bowl to me for a taste test.

An unfortunate series of events occurred on Jared's way to the rocking chair. My cat, who already had a strained relationship with my husband, jetted in front of him. Jared tripped over the cat, causing the bowl of ranch dressing to fly out of his hands and up in the air. Then, like a scene from a classic slap-stick comedy, the upended bowl landed on the cat. He was already alarmed at being stepped on, and now his fluffy orange fur was covered with creamy ranch dressing. He let out a shriek, shook his body fervently, ran a few steps and shook again, repeating this until he'd shaken all the dressing off his fur . . . and onto the carpets, the couch, the television, Jared, me and the now-wide-awake and alert baby in my arms. Even after scrubbing everything, the living room—and the cat—smelled of parsley and onion for days.

> If after first seeking God's love, comfort and wisdom there is still need to process, pray about the right person to talk to.

When we get tripped up in life, our instinct is often the same as a cat caught in a downpour. In reaction to the discomfort, sometimes even a painful shock, we try to shake it off of us and onto something else. This can take many forms — grumpiness, lashing out, disconnecting, gossip, self-medicating and one of the most dangerous forms, venting. What I've found, though, is that when I do the defensive shakeoff, I make my pain bigger. When I project my problems onto everyone around me, my problem gets larger. It's reflected back to me everywhere I look: in my husband's hurt eyes, in my child's attention-hungry tantrums, in my protective friend's brash comments to the person who "done me wrong." When we start shaking our problems onto others, a small conflict between two people becomes much, much bigger.

My first instinct when I'm angry or upset is to call a friend or family member and "talk it out." After venting or fuming or snapping at an innocent bystander, we might feel better. But those around us generally don't. Angry people tend to overshare, telling secrets or intimate things about the person who hurt them, things the recipient can't unhear.

Unless you are in an abusive or dangerous situation (in which case, confide in a safe friend, counselor or authority figure immediately), pause to consider how your reaction may affect those around you. It is okay, for a little while, to let yourself feel and process anger and hurt, despite its discomfort. It's often in these times that we grow closest to God and learn the most about ourselves and about him.

While processing painful events with a friend can be an important aspect of healing, before we do so we must ask ourselves these questions: "Am I asking this person to carry my problem for me? Is this gossip? If I share this, what good might come of it? Can I wait a day or maybe a week to see if the anger has diminished on its own? Is there someone I can talk to, perhaps a neutral counselor or wise mentor, who might be a better choice than 'shaking my mess' all over my family or a mutual friend?"

Most important, we must ask ourselves, "Have I prayed about this yet?" If after first seeking God's love, comfort and wisdom there is still need to process, pray about the right person to talk to—someone who can hear and help without getting covered with the mess as well.

PRAY

That you will be slow to anger and quick to forgive.

That when you feel angry or hurt, you will react slowly and
cautiously, rather than shaking if off on others.

That when you are hurting, you will first seek God's love, comfort
and wisdom.

REFLECT

What unresolved anger do you need to work through?

Your ways are bigger, God. Your ways are better. Your ways bring understanding if I will listen and release control. Please soften my heart, bring me to repentance, and open my eyes to your wondrous plan.

MONTH   DAY   YEAR

GOD SIGHTINGS

SCRIPTURE I AM MEMORIZING

WHAT AM I LISTENING TO?

Artist:

Song:

Playlist:

WHAT IS HAPPENING IN MY LIFE?

WHAT IS HAPPENING IN THE WORLD?

Safe in God's Hands, Not Yours

RACHEL RANDOLPH

By the time I was 18, my first 2 boyfriends had died.

My first boyfriend, Justin was kind and shy. Even after we broke up we remained good friends. Then my brother married Justin's sister. So many hearts broke when Justin, only 19, was killed in a head-on collision.

My second boyfriend, Josh, was the first boy I truly loved. And the first to break my heart. Even so, Josh remained a dear friend. He was the first to call me after Justin died, to make sure I was okay.

Then, while away at college a year later, I received an early morning phone call from my dad. "Rach, we lost Josh last night. He drowned in the lake."

The lake. Josh and I both grew up in homes on the edge of this lake, practically neighbors. I could have filled that lake with my sorrow.

This is when the idea that death was following me began to creep into my thoughts — that somehow I was a curse, and that just knowing me could lead to untimely demise. It didn't help that in the years following, about every 6 months, I found myself at the funeral of yet another young friend. In fact, I once attended 4 funerals in one year, all of them for friends under the age of 25. The secret fear grew. I would walk into funerals, afraid someone would see the black cloud above my head and shout, "She's the one causing all this! No one get close to her!"

Though I battled fear, God still came near in deeply personal ways. After Josh died, when I sat trembling, knees pulled to my chest, crying into the lake that took him, I felt strong, divine arms wrap around me.

The losses taught me the fragility of life, but also, the reality of God's presence. In time, I understood that I was not a curse, that death was not my fault. That this earth, even with its beauty, is terribly broken. It is not heaven yet.

I still struggled, however, with a heightened sense of anxiety. I knew all too well that loved ones could be gone in an instant, devastating our worlds, and I was not experiencing the peace spoken of in Daniel 10:18. Instead, I felt like the Daniel who said, "My strength is gone and I can hardly breathe" (10:17).

Eventually I met and fell in love with Jared. When he asked me to marry him,

I was thrilled but also terrified. I knew losing someone I loved this much would be unbearable.

A month before we were to marry, our pastor was preaching and asked, "When you say, 'God, my life is yours,' what is that one thing you hold back?" Immediately I knew that my *one thing* was Jared. I couldn't hear the thought of death following me here. Not here, not in my marriage.

The next day, Jared fell from a ladder, suffering a serious brain injury. In the ICU waiting room, in the wee hours, I wept, praying, "Okay, my life is yours . . . even Jared. I trust that even in this, your love is enough. Even if death follows me here, you are still good, and you will get me through even this." I clung to the words the angel spoke to Daniel: "Do not be afraid . . . Peace! Be strong" (verse 19).

By grace, Jared healed completely, and we married a month later as planned. We've been married six years now, we have a beautiful son, and life has been very, very good. A few years ago, I came across a ceramic model of two hands together, palms opened toward heaven. It sits on my mantel, and when I feel fear creeping in, I look at those hands, open my own palms, and pray, "God, I'm having trouble believing that if this bad thing were to happen, I would be okay, that you would be enough. Help my unbelief. I open my hands and give you everything." And I cling to the peace he has promised me.

I cling to the peace he has promised me.

Lord, I give my fears to you. Though I tend to worry, though my heart is anxious, you promise to carry me and give me peace no matter what this life brings. I trust you with my loved ones, with my future, and with my heart. Amen.

PRAY

That you will give God every area of your life, especially the thing that you most fear losing.

That you will trust in God's goodness and believe that the ones you love most are safer in God's hands than in yours.

That you will experience his peace.

REFLECT

What are you afraid to give to God?

MONTH   DAY   YEAR

GOD SIGHTINGS

SCRIPTURE I AM MEMORIZING

WHAT AM I LISTENING TO?

Artist:

Song:

Playlist:

WHAT IS HAPPENING IN MY LIFE?

WHAT IS HAPPENING IN THE WORLD?

The trumpeters and musicians joined in unison to give praise and thanks to the Lord. Accompanied by trumpets, cymbals and other instruments, the singers raised their voices in praise to the Lord and sang:

"He is good;
His love endures forever."
Then the temple of the Lord was filled with the cloud, and the priests could not perform their service because of the cloud, for the glory of the Lord filled the temple of God.

2 CHRONICLES 5:13-14

The Gift of Words

SHAUNA NIEQUIST

Every band should have a bass player like Nathan, and every person should have a friend like Nathan. As a musician, he's that perfect mix of really talented and totally low-key. He's always prepared, always ready to play, and—crucial for a bass player especially—he knows when to play and when to let the spaces and silences create the groove he's looking for.

As my husband, Aaron, worked on the band's calendar for the next few months, he realized that they were about to schedule a rehearsal on Nathan's birthday, so we planned a birthday dinner for him after they rehearsed.

I've been feeding musicians since I met my Aaron, and I find them some of my favorite people to feed. I love that we have a steady stream of musicians in our home, a community of people who believe that art and creativity and soul really matter, that making something out of nothing and telling your story—through lyrics or essays or anything at all—is noble work.

Some, of course, absolutely live the stereotype of starving artist, so I've gotten used to packing up every last bit of leftovers and sending them with skinny guitar players and drummers, feeling maternal and knowing in all reality I'll never see that container again. And musicians tend to be sense-oriented people, so they notice texture and smell and flavor—the most fun people to feed, of course.

That night we ate and talked and laughed. We told stories—best shows we've ever been to, songs that moved us, venues they'd love to play someday. Then the birthday toasts began—each person came ready to say something about what Nathan had brought to their life in the last year or a prayer for the year to come. Nathan is the kind of person who is encouraging people all the time—in between songs at rehearsal, in the green room, in conversation. He has a warm, easygoing presence, and people love to be around him. But he's definitely more comfortable encouraging someone else or making a fuss about someone else than being the center of attention.

The heart of hospitality is creating space for these moments, protecting that fragile bubble of vulnerability and truth and love.

At first when we were sharing, I felt his nervousness, like he wanted us to stop, like he wanted to shift attention to someone else or something else. But we stayed with it, gentle pressure, stories and prayers and words of gratitude.

The heart of hospitality is creating space for these moments, protecting that fragile bubble of vulnerability and truth and love. It's all too rare that we tell the people we love exactly why we love them—what they bring to our lives, why our lives are richer because they're in it. We do it best, I think, with our nuclear family—most of us tell our children and spouses easily and often how much we love them. But that night was an unusual and very beautiful thing: we risked the awkwardness of saying tender, meaningful things out loud in front of everyone, in front of our friends, trusting that those words would travel down to a very deep part of someone we cared about. I watched Nathan's face, and I watched it move from slightly nervous and uncomfortable to overwhelmed in the best possible way.

Sometimes food is the end, sometimes it's a means to an end, and sometimes you don't know which it is until it happens. But that night wasn't about the food. The food and the table and the laughter helped to create sacred space, a place to give someone the gift of words. That's what the night was about: sacred space and words of love.

> **Sometimes food is the end, sometimes it's a means to an end, and sometimes you don't know which it is until it happens.**

PRAY

That you will be intentional about creating community where
you are.

That you will encourage the people around you.

REFLECT

Who are the people that you love to feed and create space for?

Lord, please guide me in creating closeness and community wherever I go. When vulnerability brings me fear, guide me in embracing the gentle and open words that will knit hearts together in you. Thank you, Lord.

MONTH   DAY   YEAR

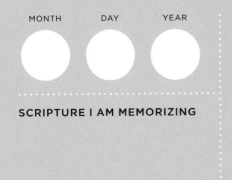

GOD SIGHTINGS

SCRIPTURE I AM MEMORIZING

WHAT AM I LISTENING TO?

Artist:

Song:

Playlist:

WHAT IS HAPPENING IN MY LIFE?

WHAT IS HAPPENING IN THE WORLD?

"There are six days when you may work, but the seventh day is a day of sabbath rest, a day of sacred assembly. You are not to do any work; wherever you live, it is a sabbath to the LORD."

LEVITICUS 23:3

Slowing Down in a World That's Gaining Speed

TSH OXENREIDER

When my family and I lived in Turkey a few years ago, we witnessed a pace of life we thought only existed half a century ago. A neighbor invited us over to their home at 2 P.M. on a Sunday. And before we could say "baklava," we were all cramming into their car like clowns, headed for a teahouse down on the Aegean Sea shoreline.

Our afternoon was spent lingering over hot çay, sugar cubes, laughing children, and words mangled somewhere between two languages, adults laughing as we attempted conversation like toddlers. We would sip tea down by the water for hours, with no agenda, no rush to the next better thing, the red-fire sunset ablaze over Mediterranean waters.

Life was . . . slower. Savored.

It wasn't perfect, of course. There were many challenges to living cross-culturally, and a slower pace of life didn't compensate for the complexities of hovering somewhere between a natively Western worldview and Eastern mores.

But still, it was fascinating to experience life in the slow lane surrounded by electricity, subway systems, and fluorescent-lit grocery aisles. It was indeed possible to live slower in the twenty-first century, so we learned.

Fast-forward years later, and we're well immersed back into our North American life. Smartphones were released sometime when we were abroad, so when we moved back, I saw many loved ones' tops of their heads for the first time. People were absorbed in their handhelds, their heads, the four walls of their houses.

Eyes freshly opened, I saw there was a direct correlation between an obsession with self and an exhausting pace of life. Centering an entire day on productivity or effectiveness as a goal equaled very little focus on other people or relationships.

His world was slow when he fully touched earth, so that we could be wholly alive and whole with God.

Jesus, of course, poured himself out as an offering. His world was slow when he fully touched earth, so that we could be wholly alive and whole with God. He is the embodiment, the very manifestation of sacrifice—the giving of self for other people. His agenda wasn't on getting things done. And as a follower of his, I want to be like that too.

I want this so fervently—so why is it so hard to shift my focus, my center, my default, to other people? Why does it feel like a burning of my flesh and a rewiring of my brain to give up my to-do list in order to make time for people?

I want to put relationships first. Hearts before agendas. Lives ahead of schedules.

I want to die to my productivity, so I can truly be with people. And I have to remind myself daily that slowing down matters.

It matters because then I can hear people. It's absolutely essential, really.

The more crammed our schedules, the less time we have to give others. When we only allow nooks and crannies in our days for rest, time alone, and self-care, then we are left threadbare to love others when they most need it. When our calendars are scribbled out in the margins because they are too full, we have no way to empty ourselves out in sacrifice.

If we want to put others first, like Jesus did, then we must. slow. down. It's the only way we can survive, thrive, be who we are meant to be in this rapid, rapid world.

If we want to put others first, like Jesus did, then we must. slow. down.

My mind drifts back frequently to our life in the Middle East. Sure, my glasses are rose-colored, but what I remember most is how I felt. I felt . . . slower. More contemplative. More at rest with myself and those put purposely around me. There, we could equate our life's measure not by boxes filled with pencil scratches but by how much freedom in our days we had to linger over çay with neighbors. With people. In relationship.

I think a slow life can happen anywhere, in any culture.

But it's harder, and it requires swimming upstream, when we live in one where the default setting is lightning fast.

And we have to be vigilantly aware of this so that our fingers continually twist the dial on our life to slower, slower, slower.

A slower-paced life isn't just a good idea, or hip, or wishful thinking. It's essential if we want to have time to be the body of Christ.

PRAY

That you will take time to put relationships first.

That you will look to Jesus' example of how he lived his life.

REFLECT

How can you make space for a slow life?

The world today values
speed and activity.
Lord, please help me
today to take a breath,
to embrace slowness,
and to love others the
way Jesus loved during
his time on earth. Amen.

MONTH   DAY   YEAR

GOD SIGHTINGS

SCRIPTURE I AM MEMORIZING

WHAT AM I LISTENING TO?

Artist:

Song:

Playlist:

WHAT IS HAPPENING IN MY LIFE?

WHAT IS HAPPENING IN THE WORLD?

The Most Epic Love Story of All Time

KATIE HARDEMAN

The man I once thought I was going to marry is engaged to someone else. I found out through Instagram, and seeing her radiant smile and shiny ring instantly transported me to the Denny's parking lot where Gregg ended things between us. He said there wasn't enough chemistry. I heard, "You're not enough." Strangely, it was in the middle of this tearful goodbye that I heard from God more clearly than I ever had. While Gregg and I embraced and lamented the end of a ten-year friendship, the following thought blew in like a cool breeze: "I have something better for you both."

Fast-forward three years and there was Gregg's "something better" staring back at me. And she was stunning. I shed salty tears that night because Gregg's future seemed so certain but mine still did not. I cried because he wanted someone else and nobody wanted me. Unwanted.

Forgotten. Ignored. Lies from the pit of hell, but I couldn't see it then.

The day after the Instagram post, I hashed things out with God. "I know you love me, Jesus, but right now that doesn't feel like enough. I know I am your beloved, but I don't feel wanted by anyone, not even you. Please remind me that you want me. That you chose me. That you are pursuing me."

That night I was given a book as a gift and could only laugh at the title. *Pursued: God's Divine Obsession with You.* I knew in my head that I was loved and pursued by God, but in my moment of weakness and in the darkness of doubt, I desperately needed to hear it from him.

In Deuteronomy 4, the chapter preceding the Ten Commandments, Moses writes of God's love for his people, who needed to be reminded that they were chosen and loved and rescued by a merciful, awesome God before they could trust and obey him. Like the nation of Israel, I need to remember that God is near to me when I pray (see Deuteronomy 4:7), that he speaks to me (4:12), that he will be found when I seek him (4:29), and that he will never abandon or forget me (4:31).

> I need to remember that God is near to me when I pray.

Some days God doesn't feel near. Sometimes I feel abandoned and forgotten. But then I am reminded that even when I don't feel pursued, he is still going before me, fighting for me, and carrying me through the wilderness "as a father carries his son" (Deuteronomy 1:31).

Moses told the Israelites to "watch yourselves closely so that you do not forget the things your eyes have seen or let them fade from your heart" (Deuteronomy 4:9). He knew it would be a struggle to remember God had rescued them, and Moses foresaw they would forget God's love when life grew dark and confusing.

I must look in God's Word to remember that his love never fails, and he never leaves.

It is in the middle of those dark and confusing times that the Enemy's lies that I am unwanted and unlovable sound like truth. It is then that I must look in God's Word to remember that his love never fails, and he never leaves. When the doubts creep in, I must remember the times he has whispered hope and pursued me when I felt alone. While my love story doesn't end in a lonely Denny's parking lot, it is part of God's grand pursuit of me.

PRAY

That God will open your eyes to the daily reminders of his love
   and pursuit.

That he will teach you to trust him when you don't feel him.

That he will reveal his love to you through his Word.

REFLECT

How have you reacted when you haven't felt pursued by God?

Lord, I feel far from you today. Life has beaten me down, and I am tired. Please be near. Please remind me of your closeness in every moment—even when I can't feel it—and help me to trust in you.

MONTH   DAY   YEAR

SCRIPTURE I AM MEMORIZING

GOD SIGHTINGS

WHAT AM I LISTENING TO?

Artist:

Song:

Playlist:

WHAT IS HAPPENING IN MY LIFE?

WHAT IS HAPPENING IN THE WORLD?

Peanut Butter Restitution

RACHEL RANDOLPH

I dropped my son off in the nursery and handed the workers his lunch box. "It contains peanut butter," I instructed, "so please don't let him near Caleb when he's eating, okay?" Then I headed toward the church lobby to meet some other moms before we headed out to a luncheon together.

I immediately eyed Caleb's mom sitting in the group, and suddenly I was flooded with guilt. I had to tell her. It was only fair for her to know I'd just sent a lethal weapon into the nursery. "I am so sorry. I packed Jackson a peanut butter sandwich. I told the staff and they know to keep the boys apart while they eat and to wipe everything down when they are done."

She was gracious. "It's okay. I'm sure it will be fine." But I knew there had to be some worry behind that statement. Though our nursery doesn't have a No Peanuts rule, I knew her son had a severe peanut allergy. I had been on a crazy writing deadline and had almost no groceries in the house. I did try to come up with something edible and nutritious that didn't contain nuts, but I found nothing. Nada. I probably should have made a quick grocery store run or dashed through a drive-thru to grab something edible and non-nut-infested, even if it meant being late for the luncheon. But the easiest, quickest option was a peanut butter sandwich.

Thankfully, Caleb was fine. The nursery workers were extra careful to keep him clear of the peanut force field. But the feeling that I had been in the wrong wouldn't go away. I texted my friend later that night. "That was so selfish and careless of me. I want you to know I'm so very sorry, and I will never do that again." It's not that packing a peanut butter sandwich in your kid's lunch is some terrible sin. But I knew my friend's fears. I knew how she worried when she left Caleb places. I knew I was one of the few friends who understood the severity of his allergies, whom she had trusted to care for her son in the past. She had even given me instructions on the EpiPen, for goodness' sake. When we know someone's fears, their hot buttons that, when pressed, can send them into the emotional equivalent of anaphylactic shock, it is a trust and a privilege. With that privilege comes a responsibility. We can no longer act as if we don't know the little things that give our friends a feeling of peace and security. Because we do know.

> When we know someone's fears, their hot buttons that, when pressed, can send them into the emotional equivalent of anaphylactic shock, it is a trust and a privilege.

Relationships are beautiful and messy like that. The more we know, the more we have to grow. As people let us in on their struggles, insecurities, or fears, they are showing us their vulnerabilities. They took a risk by sharing tender and fragile places with us, and the loving and kind response is to be a safe, compassionate, and trustworthy friend to them.

I'm learning to listen to that little twinge, that feeling in the pit of my stomach that says, Oh, that didn't feel right. I shouldn't have done or said that. I've discovered this is often the prompting of the Holy Spirit saying, "You hurt someone, and even though it feels like a small thing, it matters to them and to me. Why don't you take a moment and tend to their heart and make things right?"

Real relationships are rooted in humility.

When we hurt others, we are hurting ourselves on some level too. Often we don't set out to hurt another; we just blurt something before we realize how it could be interpreted, or we forget something that was important to a friend, or in a hurried moment find ourselves snapping at our husband or children. We don't mean to do it. And yet, sometimes, despite our best intentions, we do. When we hurt someone else, if we are sensitive to God's prompting, we will feel an "ouch" in our own gut and move to apologize.

Real relationships are rooted in humility, in the ability to say, "I'm so sorry. I was insensitive. I'll try very hard not to do that again." And then we move forward and do better the next time.

I know I have caused hurt
to others. Lord, soften
my heart. Open my eyes
to the places where I can
alter my actions, where
I can seek humility, and
where I need to ask for
forgiveness. Thank you
for forgiving me.

PRAY

That you will be aware of the way your words and actions affect others.

That you will have humility when you hurt someone, even unintentionally.

That your relationships will become richer and deeper in your willingness to recognize and reconcile all wrongs . . . no matter the size.

REFLECT

What might your relationships look like if you made a habit of always making right even the smallest of wrongs?

MONTH   DAY   YEAR

GOD SIGHTINGS

SCRIPTURE I AM MEMORIZING

WHAT AM I LISTENING TO?

Artist:

Song:

Playlist:

WHAT IS HAPPENING IN MY LIFE?

WHAT IS HAPPENING IN THE WORLD?

And the LORD has declared this day that you are his people, his treasured possession as he promised, and that you are to keep all his commands. He has declared that he will set you in praise, fame and honor high above all the nations he has made and that you will be a people holy to the LORD your God, as he promised.

DEUTERONOMY 26:18-19

Can We Talk Later?

CHIKE CHUKUDEBELU

In my life, I often fight the feeling of being overwhelmed. I've never been one to shy away from hard work. Working in a creative field means that task items often bleed beyond a typical 9 to 5 work schedule. When the juices start flowing, I've got to go with it, and it doesn't even feel like work. That's how I've lived for much of my life, and I really like it that way.

As I moved along in my career, my need for God grew. I knew that if I was going to execute my work with some level of excellence, I'd need him and his favor on my side. So I prayed, I fasted, and I went to church. I built in the action steps to make sure I was checking off all the necessary Christian boxes . . . so that I'd be blessed.

Working in a field where most things are subjective with no absolutes can be both a blessing and a curse. When you see eye to eye with colleagues, there's an amazing harmony that you can operate in. You may not know how you got there, but you never want to leave. But when your ideas bristle against someone who doesn't see things your way, you can find yourself in a fog of confusion about how you got there and especially about how to get out.

I've spent a lot of time in that fog. It's as if your whole career track is left to the whim of someone who sees you as enemy number one. You can make efforts to win that person over, but usually they backfire. For me the stress of the situation increased my anxiety, making me even more panicky. My problem-solving abilities dried up.

And all this time, I'm checking my Christian boxes: pray, fast, tithe—but nothing is changing.

I have a lot of faith in my ability to solve problems, but I didn't know what to do when I did my best work and nothing improved. I prayed, but if I'm honest, I have to admit that my prayers were, "Lord, this is what I'm going to do. Please bless it and make this solution work. Amen." They were rushed prayers. Check-box prayers.

I told myself I didn't have time to luxuriate in his presence. I had stuff to do.

But my best methods failed me. I was ashamed and quietly angry with God for not intervening. Here I was working hard to make things right, but the snapshot of my life looked so wrong. And because I was so busy I started resenting people who had time to relax on the weekends. My time with God had become cursory check-ins with me telling him to make my stuff work. I didn't get a response.

It took me coming to the end of myself and all my myriad of solutions to come to God in my brokenness and admit that I didn't know how to fix my life. I resisted that broken feeling for so long that I never realized how much lighter I'd feel once I surrendered. My pride had kept me solving problems, checking off boxes. I kept busy. And I was also wasting my time.

But when I got intentional about my quiet time, settled and still, he slowly and immediately began to heal all of my wounds. He turned around every single one of my problems in ways I had absolutely nothing to do with. He was patient with me. God loved me and wanted me to walk in obedience to him. He wanted me to listen to him.

> God loved me and wanted me to walk in obedience to him.

He knew this surrendered place was new territory for me, so he gave me time to find it. When I finally did, he wasn't angry with me for taking so long to get there. He just said, "Is now a good time to talk?" I'd been the one avoiding a serious conversation. I used my busyness as an excuse to answer with, "Can we talk later?"

Everything changed when later finally became now.

Lord, my desire for control often overshadows what I know to be true—that I am not in control at all! Please help me to stop before stepping in, to settle my spirit and listen for your guidance. I trust you in all things. Amen.

PRAY

That your busyness will not be an excuse to avoid God.

That you will recognize your need for God's healing of your brokenness.

That you will serve God with all your heart and all your soul.

REFLECT

Have you ever forgotten God when things have gone well for you?

MONTH   DAY   YEAR

GOD SIGHTINGS

SCRIPTURE I AM MEMORIZING

WHAT AM I LISTENING TO?

Artist:

Song:

Playlist:

WHAT IS HAPPENING IN MY LIFE?

WHAT IS HAPPENING IN THE WORLD?

Contributors:

Chike Chukudebelu, Katie Hardeman, Margaret Hogan, Denise Hildreth Jones, Shauna Niequist, Tsh Oxenreider, Rachel Randolph, and Alece Ronzino.

Shauna Niequist is the *New York Times* bestselling author of *Cold Tangerines*, *Bittersweet*, *Bread & Wine*, *Savor*, *Present Over Perfect*, and *I Guess I Haven't Learned That Yet*. She is married to Aaron, and they live in New York City with their sons, Henry and Mac.